beyond your number

an enneagram journal
to guide you forward
with greater wholeness

Type 6

Stephanie J Spencer

Certified Enneagram Coach

stephaniejspencer.com

with special thanks to

Ashley M Leusink
for graphic design and layout support
find out about her work as a spiritual director at
jesusandgin.com

Rachel McCauley
for copyediting support
find out about her work at
linkedin.com/in/rachel-d-mccauley

this journal is dedicated to

my family
who supports me, laughs with me, loves me,
and has been patient with me in the messy process
of finding my way as an enneagram coach.

my friends
who nerd out with me in enneagram conversations,
help me stay grounded and connected,
and remind me of the power of human belonging.

my clients
who teach me what it is to live as their enneagram types,
and give me wisdom to pass along
to others in my work.

Dear Reader,

Enneagram is not a personality test. It is a tool that gives insight into who we are and why we do what we do. These insights are intended to help us move forward in wholeness, freeing us from the passions and fixations of our types.

But knowing how to break out of these confines can prove difficult. We read books, listen to podcasts, follow Instagram accounts, and are left with the question, "Now what?"

The work can be daunting. This journal is meant to guide you through the forward movement of enneagram.

Its questions are designed to open space for you to see your behaviors, motivations, fears, and hopes with more clarity and compassion. The more honest we are with ourselves, the more insight we have into what practices might help us move forward in wholeness.

Growth is more like a wide and rocky river to navigate than a narrow set of steps to climb. Two people who are the same enneagram type may need to focus on vastly different areas of change. Our paths toward greater wholeness will be as diverse and unique as our backgrounds. Therefore, this journal is meant to be worked through as a winding path, taking you where you believe you need to go. It is not a fixed path from Point A to Point B.

The place where one person begins could be an ending place for another. The work you have already done might be the work someone else needs to begin.

I hope you will look through this journal, and allow questions to "rise from the page." The question that sticks out to you now is the one to sit with today. Answer it. Let a new question rise off the page when you are ready. Go at your own pace. Stay with a question as long as necessary: a day, a week, or a month. There isn't a right or a wrong pace.

However you engage with this journal, I hope it helps you on your journey of becoming the best version of you.

In hope,
Stephanie

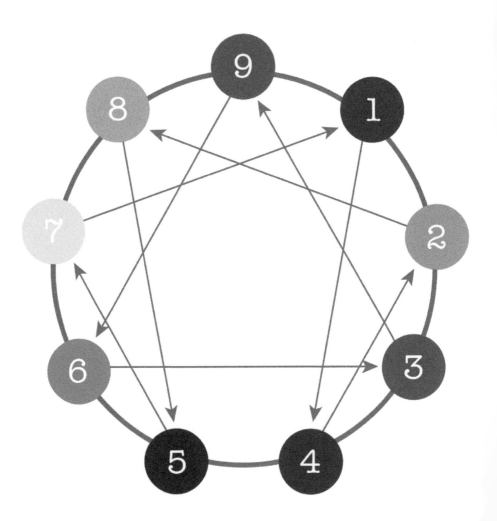

an enneagram overview

Enneagram is a framework that gives us insight into nine primary ways people engage in the human experience. These nine numbers are the enneagram types. The symbol that holds these numbers is a visual picture of the energy and interaction of the types. It is a framework that holds both complexity and unity, allowing us to be both a lot like other people and uniquely ourselves.

The circle reminds us we are all connected. We hold and display all numbers to some extent. However, we rest in one number as our home-base.

Our home-base enneagram type is the lens through which we see and experience the world.

When we know our type, we find language for the underlying factors that motivate us. We think about things like what we are afraid of, what we desire, and what makes us feel vulnerable. Knowing our enneagram number helps us name our shadows with compassion and take steps to live more deeply into our gifts.

No enneagram type is better or worse than another type. This is why numbers are more helpful than titles. As soon as we add words, there are things we do and don't want to be.

All nine enneagram types carry important facets of what it means to be human.

Each type is more of a spectrum than a point. We draw on the numbers next to our type as well, often drawing on one more strongly than the other. These adjacent numbers are called our wings.

Numbers connected to us by lines reflect our movement toward other types. In stressful states, we move with the arrow, compelled toward behaving like that type. In relaxed or secure states, we move against the arrow, opening to receiving the energy of the other type moving toward us.

Our enneagram number and its connected points are all important parts of who we are. We need to learn how to move in and receive the energies of each of them in order to move forward in wholeness.

recommended resources

This guided journal is meant to be a resource for those who already know their enneagram type and are familiar with the system. If enneagram is new to you, or you want to learn more, here are some places to explore.

websites

integrative9.com

enneagraminstitute.com

drdaviddaniels.com

podcasts

The 27 Subtypes of the Enneagram by The Liturgists

Typology with Ian Morgan Cron

The Enneagram Journey by Suzanne Stabile

music

Atlas: Enneagram by Sleeping at Last

primers

Enneagram Spectrum of Personality Styles by Jerome Wagner

The Road Back to You by Ian Morgan Cron and Suzanne Stabile

Enneagram Magazine Issue #1

deeper dives

The Complete Enneagram by Beatrice Chestnut

The Enneagram in Love and Work by Helen Palmer

The Sacred Enneagram by Chris Heuertz

The Wisdom of the Enneagram by Don Riso and Russ Hudson

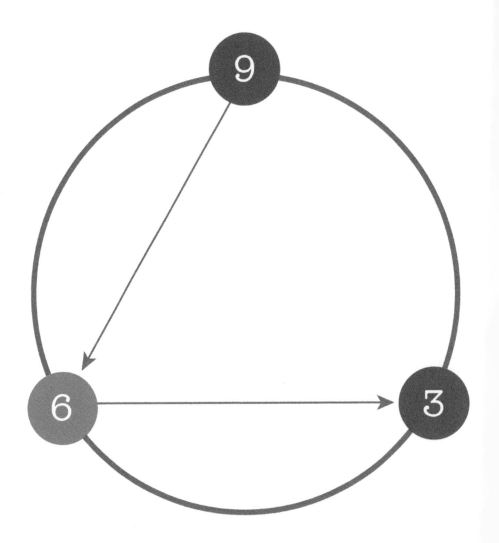

an overview of Type 6

Enneagram Type 6s are good at putting together puzzles. Whether it a family, system, or project, they can see how all the pieces fit together, and want to keep everything in place. They are reliable, trustworthy, and hard working. Their ability and desire to see how things fit can also lead to a focus on what doesn't fit or could go wrong. Type 6s want to feel secure. Their brains can get sucked into holding the domino effects of choices. In response to the fear that arises from this way of thinking, 6s may be compelled to avoid, plan for, or conquer the possibilities.

As they release control, Type 6s display the virtue of courage, trusting their inner authority and holding hope in a benevolent universe.

When Type 6s feel stress, they connect with the energy of Type 3, which can look like productivity, pragmatism, or image-consciousness.

When Type 6s feel secure, they connect with the energy of Type 9, which can look like passive-aggressiveness, balance, or flexibility.

why blue?

Type 6s surveyed chose blue as a color to represent them, because of its connection to loyalty, one of their key characteristics.

Blue is the color of both sky and sea, giving it a feeling of stability and constancy, two attributes felt in the reliability of healthy Type 6s. It is calming color, a good energy for the more anxious type sixes to absorb. Blue is often used to represent trust, wisdom, and faith.

Too much blue can come across as cold or dampen people's spirits, something catastrophizing Type 6s should be mindful of in themselves.

Type 6s are part of the Compliant Triad, along with the Type 1s (gray) and Type 2s (green). These three types are responsible with follow-through and are dedicated to the groups of which they are part. Each of their colors have a coolness and neutrality that goes well with many other colors.

When Type 6s feel secure, they access the purple of Type 9. Purple contains both warm and cool properties, a balance needed in Type 6. Purple is also a royal color, that can remind 6s to trust their own authority.

"Supposing a tree fell down, Pooh, when we were underneath it?"

"Supposing it didn't," said Pooh after careful thought.

Piglet was comforted by this.

A.A. Milne, Winnie-the-Pooh

Enneagram is a map and a guide.
It does not describe the entire geography of the human landscape. It is meant to help us grow in awareness and move towards health and wholeness. It is not intended to hold every nuance and attribute of a human person.
I am an enneagram type.
I am ALSO a unique individual.

In what ways does enneagram Type 6 describe me?

In what ways does enneagram Type 6
not describe me?

How can I keep the tensions between my uniqueness
and enneagram Type 6 in mind as I do this work?

Are there any potential barriers keeping me from
doing the work of the enneagram?

Can I remove some of these barriers
before diving deeper?

What resources do I need in order to engage in the work of the enneagram? (i.e. intentional time)

Are there concrete supports that would help me move forward? (i.e. a friend with whom to process)

What is making me feel vulnerable, defensive, or afraid right now?

Do any of these things need to be resolved before moving forward with this journal?

Can I look at my habits with compassion
and choose to change them to reflect the values
true to my essence?

What might keep me from seeing myself with hope,
possessing the potential for change?

Can I use the enneagram as a tool to become more embodied and present to my life and relationships?

Can I keep this posture and goal in mind as I keep moving forward?

Are there ways I am trapped within
my enneagram type?

How do I need to recognize the transformation I have
already done before beginning the work of this
journal?

words that can be
used to describe Type 6

cooperative   vigilant   ambivalent

cautious   prepared   suspicious

dutiful   committed   doubting

worrying   responsible   honorable

rigid   indecisive   conscientious

loyal   catastrophizing   loyal

devil's advocate   rule-follower   projecting

rule-challenger   skeptical   insightful

respectful   traditional   timid

dogmatic   tenacious   truthful

What are three words I like?

What are three words I don't like?

What are three words that once
described me but no longer do?

What are three words that describe me now?

Fear is the cheapest room in the house.
I would like to see you living in better conditions.

Hafiz

on thinking

What am I afraid would happen if I didn't map
the contingency plan and worst-case scenarios?

How much energy do I expend planning for possibilities
that never come to pass?

When has my questioning mind provided clarity?

When has it made paralyzed me?

Do I avoid action through thinking? How?

What could happen if I risked taking steps sooner?

How has my ability to plan and forecast helped people, organizations, and projects be successful?

How can I celebrate my contribution?

Do I think of myself more of
a pessimist or realist?

Would others describe me the same way?

Am I turning to people or things around me for reassurance and support?

What steps could I take to grow the confidence of my inner knowing?

Am I afraid of being betrayed? By who or what?
How often do I feel this fear?

Would my actions change if I believed others
would not let me down?

What does it take for me to trust authority?

When have my suspicions of leaders been proven true?
When have leaders exceeded my expectations?

Has my ability to see motives and agendas been a positive influence in my relationships and work?

Has this skill had a negative influence?

Has my loyalty to others helped them?
Has it helped me? How?

Are there ways my loyalty has hurt me or others?

on loyalty

When have I shown commitment to something or someone I believed in? How has this provided the unseen support to keep things moving forward?

Can I see my worth to them?

Do I have a devotion to my own well-being that matches my devotion to the well-being of others?

How would my life be different if I had a greater commitment to fulfilling my own needs and desires?

How often do I say or think, "Yes, but…"?
What would happen if I gave more energy to
the "yes" than the "but"?

Do I believe that my work could be successful
and thrive? Why or why not?

How can I develop greater confidence about
my talent and potential?

I want to think again
of dangerous and noble things.
I want to be light and frolicsome.
I want to be improbable beautiful
and afraid of nothing,
as though I had wings.

Mary Oliver

on responsibility

Has my contentment with working hard
behind-the-scenes given space for others to shine?

Has behind-the-scenes work held me back from a spotlight
that could be mine to stand in?

Has my sense of responsibility ever put more
on my plate than is healthy for me?

Am I getting overwhelmed?
Do I need to set fresh boundaries?

When has my follow-through helped a group
or project succeed?

Is there a time when I should have allowed failure instead
of picking up the dropped pieces?

How often do I try to protect people through my actions?

Do they need my protection? Why or why not?

How often does fear drive my actions?

What could help me move forward with
more courage?

Do I ever keep myself busy as a way to feel secure?
Does it work?

Has my anticipation of what might go wrong ever
kept me from experiencing the joy and goodness
of things going well?

Does my imagination increase my suspicions about what could go wrong?

Could I do something to turn this imagination in another direction?

Do I experience anxiety in my body?
Are there practices I can do to help me experience calm?

Has my readiness for danger equipped me to respond well
when a crisis hit? Were my gifts recognized in that
moment? By others? By me?

Does being caught off guard make me feel vulnerable? How does this affect my choices?

If you resonate with counterphobic Type 6:

Does my desire to prove I'm stronger than fear ever push me into unsafe situations?

How might I respond differently if desire for security wasn't driving me?

May all that is unlived in you

Blossom into a future

Graced with love.

John O'Donohue

Our first response to stress tends to be
to "double down" in our primary type.

In higher levels of stress, Type 6 moves toward Type 3.
The movement can be unhealthy or healthy,
paralyzing or resourcing.

Words that might describe a Type 3 include...
productive, successful, competent, busy, pragmatic, ambitious,
image-conscious, successful, performing, workaholic, trendy,
arrogant, outgoing, scheming, popular, recognition-seeking

When I feel stress, do I become more anxious or rigid, play devil's
advocate, feel weighed down by responsibility, or display other
stereotypical traits of Type 6?

Are there times when stress has made me feel like
a "different person"?

In stress, am I slipping into the less healthy characteristics of Type 3 and

... using busyness to distract myself from fear?

... looking for security in a role or image?

... pursuing extra projects and worked doubly hard in order to please authority or avoid failure?

In stress, am I connecting with the healthier characteristics of a Type 3 and

... focusing my energy into achieving goals and taking effective and concrete action?

... feeling confident and open to the spotlight?

... knowing my competence to move in proactive directions?

Integrating my inner Type 3 will help me move forward in wholeness.

Can I consciously open myself to the healthier characteristics of this type?

When I feel secure, I may feel or act differently than I do at other times, and even from the typical descriptions of my enneagram type.

In security, Type 6 moves toward Type 9.
The movement can be unhealthy or healthy, paralyzing or resourcing.

Words that might describe a Type 9 include...
patient, easygoing, calm, reassuring, neglectful, mediating, conflict-avoiding, tedious, stubborn, flexible, comfort-seeking, permissive, settled, distractible, supportive, grounded

Some people might feel secure on a day off, or on vacation, or at home, or with a trusted friend.

What helps me feel secure?

In security, am I slipping into the less healthy characteristics of a Type 9 and

... numbing myself from fear?

... using routine to avoid unknown situations?

... getting stuck in indecisiveness, not being able to name what I want or need?

In security, when am I connecting with the healthier characteristics of a Type 9, and...

... connecting to my inner stillness and peace?

... going with the flow and trust the process?

... seeing and integrating multiple sides of issues and problems?

Integrating my inner Type 9 will help me move forward with wholeness.

Can I consciously open myself to the healthier characteristics of this type?

We live in a world in which we need to share responsibility. It's easy to say, 'It's not my child, not my community, not my world, not my problem.'

Then there are those who see the need and respond. I consider those people my heroes.

Fred Rogers

Have I cultivated my presence to show up fully and follow my convictions without grasping for security?

Are others experiencing the virtue of courage emanating from my heart?

What are some ways I see loyalty valued and reflected in my life?

Have I made the world more trustworthy and secure through my actions? How? Where?

Do I connect with and trust my sense of
inner-knowing and authority?

How am I cultivating healthy groups and teams
through cooperation and collaboration?

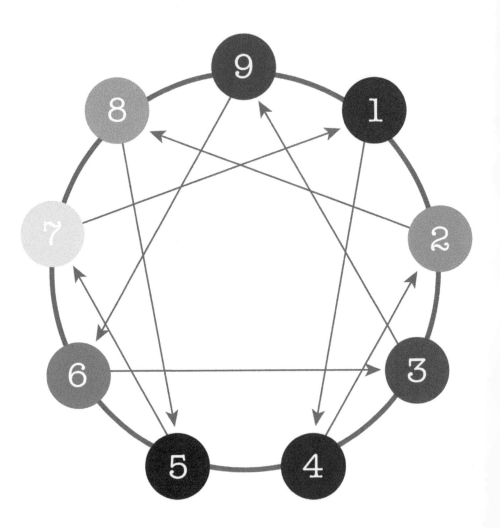

now what?

The question at the beginning of this journal re-surfaces. You have read books, listened to podcasts, perused websites, and followed Instagram accounts. Additionally, you have worked through this journal. I hope what you've written here will continue to be a reference that leads you to better, more complete versions of yourself.

But the question remains... now what?

Keep moving forward. It takes continual work to stay aware of ourselves. This world has a tendency to lull us to sleep.

Actively keep the characteristics, habits, and passions of your Type in your mind as you move through daily choices. Celebrate ways you have grown and notice where you still have room to move forward.

Take time to learn about numbers other than your own. Notice ways other Types exist in some way within you. If there is work to do there, open yourself up to it. (This may be especially useful with your stress response and security numbers.)

Ask the people in your life about their Types, and notice the similarities and differences in how you experience the world. Use enneagram as a tool to help you grow in compassion towards others.

Breathe. Be. Stay in touch with your body. Ground your questions with presence.

You may want to keep this journal to look at once or twice a year. Notice how your answers change. Celebrate the journey.

And if you get discouraged, maybe you can take with you one of my favorite quotes, from Parker Palmer,

"What a long time it can take to become the person you've always been."

From one becomer to another,
Stephanie

Lightning Source UK Ltd.
Milton Keynes UK
UKHW051139270720
367231UK00008B/101